PARASITES

Hookworms

Gail Jarrow

**KIDHAVEN
PRESS**™

THOMSON
—✷—™
GALE

San Diego • Detroit • New York • San Francisco • Cleveland
New Haven, Conn. • Waterville, Maine • London • Munich

Picture Credits

Cover: © Dr. Dennis Kunkel/Visuals Unlimited
© St. Bartholomew's Hospital/Custom Medical Stock
  Photography, 15 (left)
John Bavosi/Photo Researchers, Inc., 19
Courtesy of Richard Bungiro Phd and Michael
  Cappello MD, 8
CDC, 12 (left, below center)
CDC/Dr. Mae Melvin, 6 (insets), 26
CNRI/Photo Researchers Inc., 6 (center)

© COREL Corporation, 23
© Custom Medical Stock Photography, 11
Jan Hinsch/Photo Researchers, Inc., 5
Courtesy of Dhanpat Jain MD and Michael Cappello
  MD, 12 (bottom right)
© Dr. Dennis Kunkel/Visuals Unlimited, 17
Dr. P. Marazzi/Photo Researchers, Inc., 15 (right)
© Fred Marsik/Visuals Unlimited, 5 (left)
PhotoDisc, 23 (inset)
© Royalty Free/CORBIS, 26
Suzanne Santillan, 12

© 2004 by KidHaven Press. KidHaven Press is an imprint of The Gale Group, Inc.,
a division of Thomson Learning, Inc.

KidHaven™ and Thomson Learning™ are trademarks used herein under license.

For more information, contact
KidHaven Press
27500 Drake Rd.
Farmington Hills, MI 48331-3535
Or you can visit our Internet site at http://www.gale.com

LIBRARY OF CONGRESS CATALOGING-IN-PUBLICATION DATA

Jarrow, Gail.
  Hookworms / by Gail Jarrow.
    v. cm. — (Parasites)
Includes bibliographical references and index.
Contents: A bloodsucking parasite—Invasion of the human body—Hookworm
victims—Protecting people from hookworms.
  ISBN 0-7377-1781-5
  1. Hookworm disease—Juvenile literature. 2. Hookworms—Juvenile literature.
[1. Hookworms.] Title. II. Series.
  RC199.95.J37 2004
  616.9'654—dc21

                                                                    2003010394

CONTENTS

A Bloodsucking Parasite

Human hookworms infect more than one in five people in the world. After a hookworm invades the human body, it steadily sucks its host's blood, sometimes for several years. Some people die because of the hookworm.

Hookworms belong to the group of threadlike worms called **nematodes**, or roundworms. The parasite attacks several kinds of mammals, including humans, dogs, and cats.

Suction Cup Mouth

Inside the **small intestine**, the adult hookworm uses its specially designed mouth to feed on its host's blood. Working like a suction cup, the mouth attaches to the wall of the small intestine. The mouth contains either teeth or cutting blades, depending on the type of hookworm. As the hookworm sucks the intestinal wall into its mouth, these sharp edges tear open the host's blood vessels.

Hookworms use their sharp, bladelike teeth (below) and suction cup mouth (left) to attach to the host's small intestine and suck blood.

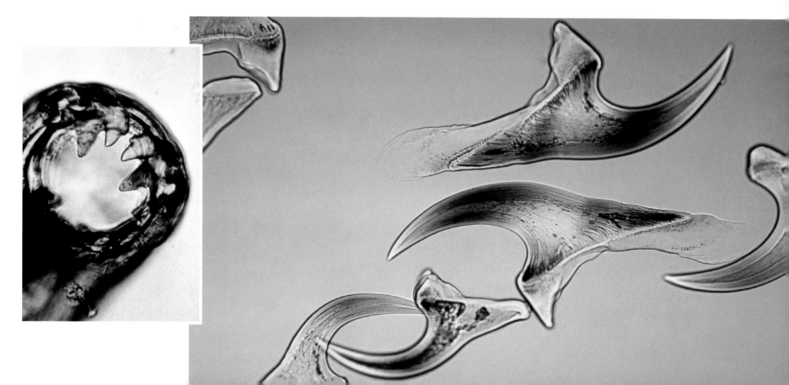

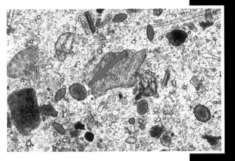

A hookworm egg (top) will hatch into a larva (below) before developing into an adult (center).

The parasite releases chemicals that stop the host's blood from clotting. Then the hookworm sucks up the blood like a vacuum cleaner. It feeds for a while at one spot on the intestinal wall, then moves to a new location.

A Permanent Guest

Once a hookworm invades its host's small intestine, it will live there for the rest of its life. This is usually one to five years, but it can be longer.

Male and female hookworms mate inside the small intestine. A female hookworm begins laying eggs about two months after it enters the host's body. Each female lays thousands of eggs a

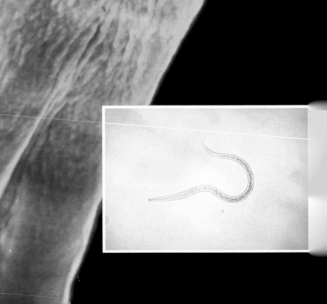

day. The eggs pass from the host mixed with **feces**, or solid waste. Hookworms may spread to new hosts if these feces are deposited on top of soil.

Within two days of leaving the host's body, the hookworm eggs hatch. The tiny, wormlike **larvae** feed on **bacteria** in the feces. This is the only time in a hookworm's life when it does not live as a parasite inside a host.

Finding a Host

The larvae do not move far from the top of the soil where they hatch. After about a week, they are ready to infect a host. With their upper bodies raised in the air, the larvae wait for a host to pass by.

When the skin of an animal or human touches a hookworm larva, the parasite climbs aboard. The larva burrows into the host's skin, using a back-and-forth body motion. Once inside the skin, the larva travels through the host's body to the small intestine. During the larva's journey, it grows and changes. When it reaches the intestine, it develops into an adult hookworm.

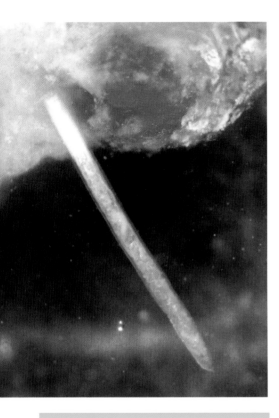

A hungry hookworm attaches to its host's intestinal wall.

Cannot Live Everywhere

During the time a hookworm larva is outside a host, it needs special conditions to survive. For an egg to hatch and the larva to develop, the soil must be shady and moist. The air temperature must be above sixty-five degrees Fahrenheit. Under these conditions, a larva can live about three to four weeks. If it does not invade a host by then, the larva will die.

Hookworms thrive in tropical and subtropical regions of the world that have warm temperatures and moist soils. Some communities in these areas have poor **sanitation** and no indoor toilets. Feces are discarded on the ground where people walk barefoot, exposing their skin to hookworm larvae.

Farmers in undeveloped countries often fertilize fields with human feces. When fieldworkers touch hookworm larvae with their hands or feet, they become infected. Eating unwashed food from these fields can also infect people with hookworms.

In these parts of the world, the human hookworm has everything it needs to survive.

CHAPTER 2

Invasion of the Human Body

At any given time, hookworms infect about 1.3 billion people throughout the world. Each year, sixty-five thousand people die because of them. In many places, the parasite is a major public health problem. People in poor areas of Asia, Latin America, Africa, and the Pacific Islands suffer the most from hookworm infections.

Human Hookworms

Two kinds of hookworms invade the human small intestine. *Necator americanus*, the New World hookworm, lives mostly in the Western Hemisphere. *Ancyclostoma duodenale*, the Old World hookworm, is most common in Europe and Asia. Both kinds are found throughout the world, however.

The two types of worms have different ways of entering the body. New World hookworm larvae can only enter through the skin. Old World hookworm larvae can enter either through the skin or through the mouth.

Hookworms enter through the mouth when people put dirty fingers in their mouth or eat food that is contaminated with feces. The Old World larvae travel the same path as food. When they reach the small intestine, they latch onto the intestinal wall.

From Skin to Small Intestine

When the hookworm burrows into the bare skin, some people develop an itchy rash at the entry point. Once inside the skin, the larva moves into the blood vessels.

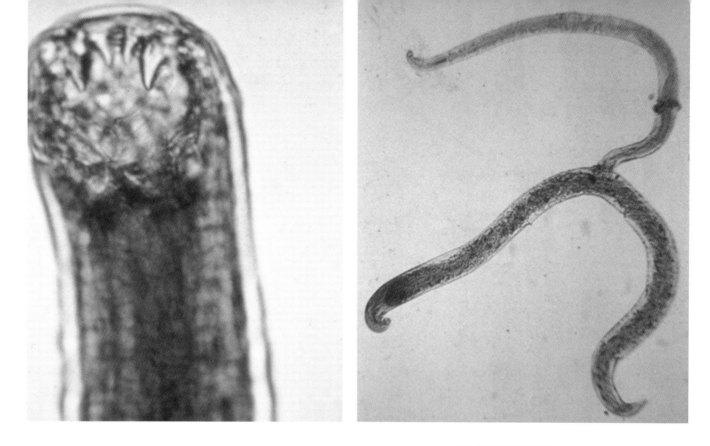

Traveling through the blood vessels, the larva reaches the heart and is pumped to the lungs. In the lungs, it passes from the blood vessels into tiny air sacs. When the person coughs, the larva is pushed up to the throat. Without knowing it, the person swallows the larva. From the throat, the larva follows the

Both the Ancyclostoma duodenale *(left) and* Necator americanus *(right) invade the human small intestine.*

Hookworm Life Cycle

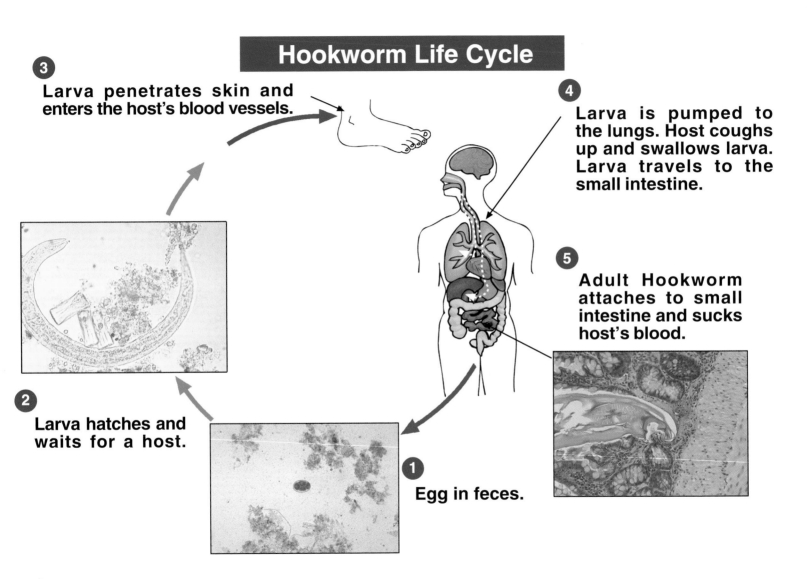

3 Larva penetrates skin and enters the host's blood vessels.

4 Larva is pumped to the lungs. Host coughs up and swallows larva. Larva travels to the small intestine.

5 Adult Hookworm attaches to small intestine and sucks host's blood.

2 Larva hatches and waits for a host.

1 Egg in feces.

same path as food and ends up in the small intestine, where it develops into an adult hookworm. This journey through the human body usually takes about a week.

Loss of Blood

The hookworm attaches to the wall of the small intestine and begins sucking blood. Many people never feel sick from a hookworm infection. Others develop diarrhea, pain in the abdomen, and blood in the feces. They may not feel like eating.

People who become sick from hookworms are usually carrying dozens of them. In heavy infections, a person carries several hundred hookworms that suck up as much as a cup of blood each day. Old World hookworm infections are more serious because each worm sucks up to ten times more blood than a New World hookworm.

The loss of blood can cause **anemia**, making a person feel weak. Severe anemia can damage the heart. When children lose blood from hookworm infections, they do not grow and develop normally.

People of all ages who have hookworm infections are more likely to get sick from other diseases.

Attacks by Dog and Cat Hookworms

Dog and cat hookworms can also infect people. The larvae of these hookworms enter humans through the skin, but they usually cannot travel past the skin layers. The larvae tunnel through the skin for weeks, causing an itchy rash that looks like wiggly red lines. This hookworm infection is called **creeping eruption**.

Creeping eruption usually occurs in warm, moist climates where the young hookworm larvae can survive outside a host. People are infected when their skin touches soil or sand containing dog or cat feces. This often happens in sandboxes or on beaches. In the United States, creeping eruption is seen mostly in the southeastern states.

Because dog and cat hookworms stay in a person's skin and do not reach the small intestine, they do not cause the serious health problems that human hookworms do.

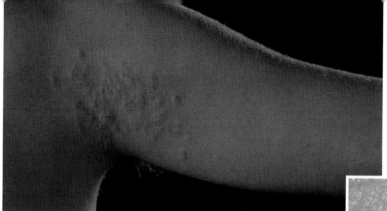

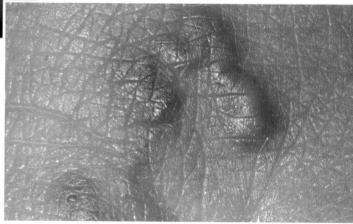

Dog and cat hookworm larvae burrow through human flesh, leaving an itchy rash called creeping eruption (shown).

A Successful Parasite

Human hookworms have adapted well to their hosts. While living in one person's body, a pair of hookworms produces millions of eggs that can spread to other people. They are successful parasites because they do not usually kill the host. In fact, hookworms can survive in the human body for several years without causing a life-threatening illness. But for those people who develop symptoms, the parasites are unwelcome visitors.

CHAPTER 3

Hookworm Victims

Most hookworm victims live in warm climates where sanitation is poor. Yet even in areas with good sanitation, people sometimes get infected.

A Mystery Illness

Doctors get their first hint that a sick person might have hookworms if the patient has anemia, diarrhea, and intestinal pain. They check the person's feces for

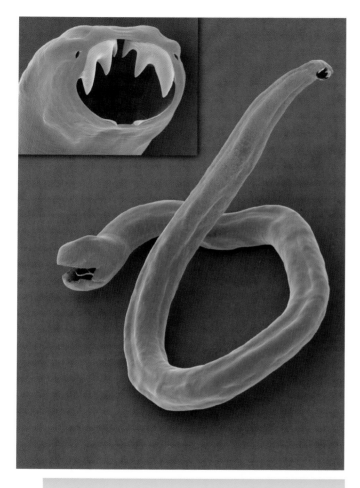

Hookworms cause serious illnesses including anemia and diarrhea.

hookworm eggs. Occasionally, doctors need to do additional detective work.

A seventy-eight-year-old man from Taiwan had complained of stomach pain for four months. Hookworm is no longer common in Taiwan, yet the man had symptoms of hookworm disease. He had anemia and blood in his feces, which are signs of blood loss from the intestines. But when doctors checked his feces for hookworm eggs, they found none.

The doctors also peered inside the man's intestines with an **endoscope**. An endoscope is a thin, flexible instrument that helps a doctor see inside certain body organs. Using the endoscope, doctors found many hookworms attached to the wall of the man's small intestine. They treated him with a drug that kills hookworms, and the man recovered.

A Vacation Souvenir

Hookworm infections sometimes come from unexpected places. Soon after a twenty-nine-year-old American man returned from vacation in Jamaica, he noticed an itchy, threadlike rash between his toes. At first his doctor thought it was athlete's foot, and he gave him a cream to heal it.

But after five days, the rash had spread to the bottom of the man's feet. The doctor took another look. When he heard that his patient had been on a Jamaican beach, he realized that the rash was creeping eruption.

The man had walked on the beach in bare feet. Hookworms, probably from dogs or cats, had invaded the skin of his feet. Because these were not human hookworms, they did not spread elsewhere in his body. A special cream killed the hookworm larvae, and his rash disappeared.

A New Problem

Researchers study human parasites throughout the world, trying to find ways to improve people's health.

In one part of Haiti, a group of researchers discovered that the number of children with hookworms was increasing. This was a surprise because hookworms had not been a problem in the community before. Although sanitation was poor, the soil had been too dry for hookworm larvae to survive.

The researchers realized that something important had changed. A channel had once prevented flooding of the nearby river. But when the government stopped taking care of it, the river often flooded. The soil in the area was now always moist, creating ideal conditions for hookworms.

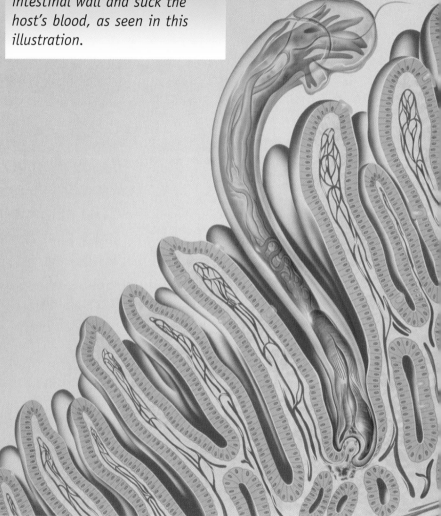

Hookworms cling to the host's intestinal wall and suck the host's blood, as seen in this illustration.

Doctors gave the people a drug that killed their hookworms, but this did not end the infections. Until the wet soils dried out and sanitation in the area improved, the people continued to be reinfected with hookworms.

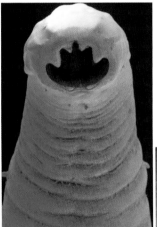

Hookworm infections (below, right) can occur wherever hookworms thrive.

Watch Where You Lie

A Florida plumber never expected to get hookworm. His doctor's news was a big shock.

The man went to his doctor when he developed an itchy rash across his back. The doctor recognized creeping eruption. Trying to figure out how his

patient became infected with hookworm larvae, the doctor asked the man about his job.

The plumber had been working without a shirt under an open crawl space of a house. To work on the pipes, he had spent time lying on his back in the dirt. He remembered seeing dog feces under the house where stray dogs had wandered.

The feces-contaminated dirt had contained dog hookworm larvae, which invaded the skin on the man's back. A drug applied to the skin killed the larvae and cured his rash. And the plumber learned a lesson about working under crawl spaces.

Humans at Risk

Where hookworms thrive, humans risk being infected by the parasites. Even after treatment to kill them, a person can be reinfected if exposed again. But people can protect themselves if they understand how the parasites attack.

CHAPTER 4

Protecting People from Hookworms

The first step in preventing hookworm infections is to keep hookworm eggs out of the soil surface. Human feces, which might contain eggs, should be disposed of. Public health workers in many rural areas of the world are helping people improve sanitation and toilets. Health experts are also encouraging farmers to stop using human feces to fertilize fields.

Hookworm infections often occur in fields (right) containing hookworm-infested soil (below).

23

The second step in preventing infections is to keep hookworm larvae away from the body. People should wear shoes in places where soil might contain human feces. This prevents larvae from entering the body at the most common site—the feet. One kind of human hookworm can infect the body if swallowed. To avoid this, people should keep dirty hands and unwashed vegetables out of the mouth.

Since dog and cat hookworms can infect humans, too, it is a good idea to wear shoes wherever dog and cat feces might be on the ground. Animals should be kept out of sandboxes where children might touch the feces. Pet owners should have dogs and cats dewormed by a veterinarian. The drugs will kill hookworms that the animals may spread to humans.

Dealing with Infections

People who are already ill are more likely to become sick from a hookworm infection. In places where hookworms are a constant

Hookworm larvae commonly infect the feet.

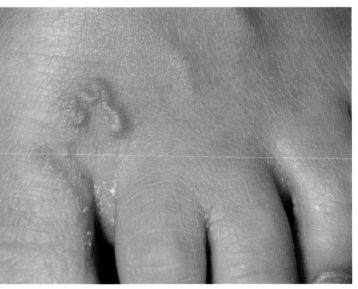

problem, public health workers try to reduce the effects of these infections by improving overall health. They encourage people to eat a better diet. They also treat illnesses caused by other intestinal parasites.

When people become sick from hookworms, doctors can cure them. Drugs have been developed that kill the hookworm larvae in the skin and the hookworm adults in the small intestine. These medicines are safe and easy to take. Once the hookworms are dead, the person's health quickly improves. Someone with anemia due to blood loss is given iron supplements to build up strength again.

A New Weapon Against Hookworm?

Despite these efforts, hookworm infections continue to be a serious health concern. Sanitation remains poor in many parts of the world, causing people to be infected again and again. Drugs used to kill hookworms give only temporary protection. A person will be reinfected whenever exposed to new hookworm

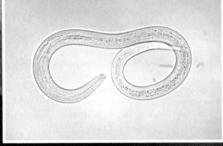

Hookworm infections are most common in undeveloped areas with poor sanitation.

larvae. Doctors have noticed that some drugs no longer work as well as they once did. This may mean that the parasite is able to resist the drugs.

To overcome these problems, researchers are looking for additional ways to protect people from hookworms. One promising idea is a **vaccine**. This would be similar to vaccines used to fight diseases such as measles, mumps, and polio.

The hookworm vaccine would be injected into a person's body. This substance would stimulate the body to fight off future hookworm infections. Researchers still have more work to do before a vaccine is ready to use on people.

Hope for the Future

Many organizations throughout the world are working to prevent and treat hookworm infections. These efforts are focused on undeveloped countries where hookworms and other parasites severely affect health. In China, Latin America, India, Southeast Asia, and Africa, hookworms infect and sicken a large part of the population.

To control hookworm, sanitation must be improved and people must be educated about how to avoid infection. Until then, more than 1 billion of the world's people will continue to be hosts to this bloodsucking parasite.

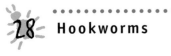

GLOSSARY

anemia: A medical condition in which a person has less than the normal amount of red blood cells. As a result, the person feels weak and has no energy.

bacteria: Microscopic organisms.

creeping eruption: The itchy, red rash caused when dog or cat hookworm larvae infect the skin of humans.

endoscope: A thin, flexible, lighted tube used to look inside the body.

feces: The solid, undigested waste eliminated from the intestines.

larva: The stage of a hookworm's development into an adult after hatching from an egg.

nematodes: The group of animals to which hookworms belong. Also called roundworms.

sanitation: Practices such as safe disposal of human waste that reduce the spread of infection and disease.

small intestine: The part of the human digestive system between the stomach and the large intestine where food is broken down and absorbed.

vaccine: A substance injected into a person's body that stimulates it to fight a certain infection.

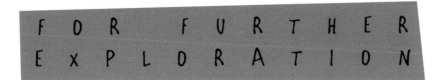

FOR FURTHER EXPLORATION

Books

Howard Facklam and Margery Facklam, *Parasites*. New York: Twenty-First Century Books, 1994. Explains how hookworms spread among people in poor rural areas of the world.

Websites

Centers for Disease Control and Prevention (www.cdc.gov). This site contains fact sheets with information about hookworm infections.

National Center for Infectious Diseases, Division of Parasitic Disease (www.dpd.cdc.gov). Check out the image library for photos of hookworms at all stages in the life cycle.

Personal M.D. (www.personalmd.com). Read an article at this site that explains how doctors diagnose and treat hookworm infections.

Sabin Vaccine Institute (www.sabin.org). Find out how researchers are working to develop a human vaccine against hookworm.

INDEX

Ancyclostoma duodenale, 10
anemia, 13

bacteria, 7
beaches, 14
blood, 10–11, 13

cat hookworms, 14, 24
creeping eruptions, 14
  infections of, 18, 20–21

diagnosis, 16–17
dog hookworms, 14, 21, 24
drugs, 25, 27

eggs, 6–7, 8, 15
endoscopes, 17

feces, 7, 8
feet, 24
fertilizer, 8
Florida, 20–21

Haiti, 19–20
hookworm types, 10, 14
hosts
  feeding on, 5–6

finding, 7
path through, 7, 10–12
types of, 4

infections
  area of most, 9
  of creeping eruption, 18, 20–21
  dealing with, 24–25
  extent of, 9, 28
  recurring, 25, 27–28
  seriousness of, 13
  site on host of, 24
  spread of, 7, 8

Jamaica, 18

larvae
  of dog and cat hookworm, 14
  drugs to kill, 25
  survival of, outside of host, 8
  travel of, inside of host, 7, 10

mating, 6–7, 15
mouth, 5

Necator americanus, 10
nematodes, 4

New World hookworms, 10

Old World hookworms, 10

prevention, 22, 24

rashes, 14
reproduction, 6–7, 15
roundworms, 4

sandboxes, 14, 24
sanitation, prevention and, 22, 28
shoes, 24
small intestine, 5
subtropical regions, 8
survival conditions
  climate and, 8
  sanitation and, 16, 19–20
symptoms, 13, 16, 17

Taiwan, 17
tropical regions, 8

United States, 14, 20–21

vaccines, 27

ABOUT THE AUTHOR

Gail Jarrow is the author of nature books, novels, and magazine articles for young readers. Before becoming an author, she taught science and math in elementary and middle schools. She received her undergraduate degree in zoology from Duke University and her master's degree from Dartmouth College. She and her husband have three children.